T0155091

WISE FISH

Tales in 6/8 Time

POEMS BY

ADRIAN CASTRO

COFFEE HOUSE PRESS

MINNEAPOLIS

Coffee House Press books are available to the trade through our primary distributor, Consortium Book Sales & Distribution, 1045 Westgate Drive, Saint Paul, MN 55114. For personal orders, catalogs, or other information, write to: Coffee House Press, 27 North Fourth Street, Suite 400, Minneapolis, MN 55401.

Coffee House Press is a nonprofit literary publishing house. Support from private foundations, corporate giving programs, government programs, and generous individuals help make the publication of our books possible. We gratefully acknowledge their support in detail in the back of this book.

Good books are brewing at coffeehousepress.org

LIBRARY OF CONGRESS CATALOGING-IN-PUBLICATION DATA
Castro, Adrian, 1967–
Wise fish : tales in 6/8 time / poems by Adrian Castro.
p. cm.
ISBN-13: 978-1-56689-172-1 (alk. paper)
ISBN-10: 1-56689-172-8 (alk. paper)
1. Africans—Caribbean Area—Poetry. 2. West Indian Americans—Poetry. 3. Caribbean Area—Poetry. 4. Miami (Fla.)—Fiction. I. Title.
PR9205.9.C37W57 2005
811'.54—DC22
2004027802

3 5 7 9 8 6 4
Printed in the United States

ACKNOWLEDGMENTS

"Hoodoo Whisper" in *Bum Rush the Page: a Def Poetry Jam;* "Para La Installation de José Bedia" and "The Mysteries Come to the Bridge" in *Renaming Ecstasy: Latino Writings on the Sacred;* "Brincando el Charco" in *Illuminations;* "One Irony of the Caribbean" in *Warpland: A Journal of Black Literature and Ideas,* and *Step into a World: A Global Anthology of New Black Literature;* "When She Carried a Calabash" in *Drumvoices Revue.*

WISE FISH
Tales in 6/8 Time

CONTENTS

THE SOUND OF LEAVING

MISA CARIBEÑA

Who gives thanks today, receives blessings of tomorrow—
Niurca, Mario, Pura, Eugenio Villar, Edouard Duval Carrié,
Charo Oquet, James Herring, Virgil Suarez,
Victor Hernández Cruz, and Quincy Troupe.
Adupe fun Isheshe—Olódùmarè, Orí mi, Òrúnmìlà,
Òshun, Ògún, Èshù. Ògbó Àtó, Ifá gba wá o.

1959—THE FIRST MASS (FOR INSTANCE)

Fue la primera misa
        where
    mass people said adios—
(my tierra: gooooo go go
    with god)
They chanted partly from
    Spanish
        another in lengua
            Lukumí, Nkama
                Lukumí, Nkama
    spilling secret requiem en la isla—
will we return another day
    (ae!   ae aeeeee!)

Mi padrino interned himself in his favorite cemetery
(the one with a siguaraya & bearded revolutionaries)
        shoveled
           with long thumbnail
               the scoop of soil & oooooh
            was it rich
      stories wrapped in scarlet leather
          leaf
        yet another possession to parade
        algo to bring in procession a-
           way
      (este exile may not have a return) he said
    At least he'll be buried
      among the soil de allá
      (eah!   eaeeeeeaaaah!)
And then we brought more
    relics
  the technique of

handrolling tabaco into small walking sticks
the poem spoken in clave
in 6/8 time
the bilingual thought
and all such lovely tricks
This is why
we arrived with integrity (in spite of
the chaos of the Florida Straits
in spite of the waves with fins that nibble at the identity)—
why we've become mostly
wise fish
(ae!   aeeeeee!)

BEFORE DEPARTURE

"How-many-
   times-
   has-this-story-been-told"
     (the story returns)
"The-wave-returns-but-departs-differently"
"We-were-one-of-many-who-left"
  These were the names
  the ones who cast divination
  when immigration first occurred
  when we were first cast
  among many who left

  Un niño de 8 años
  black trousers borrowed from fading baby tux
  white shirt washed by wind
  washed by stone también
  poverty washed too
  kisses his mother on her dripping cheek
  yet they swore separation
  wouldn't be long
  yet a certain burden burrows with this assumption

"The-wave-returns-but-
  departs-differently"
"How-many-
  times-
  has-this-story-been-told"
     (the story returns)
"We-were-one-of-many-who-left"
  Were the ones who cast divination
  when immigration first occurred
  when we were first cast
  when conspiracy was carved to float

The beach was riddled with new hope
    (it could've been a
           dock or
               airport)
The young with long bags of failure below their eyes
        many merely 20
The guard whose purple tongue was dead since the very onset
    could not deny the signs of defeat
A mirror which hung invisible like a guardian spirit
      repeating the chorus of exile or stagnation
The older ones huddled like bent cocoteros
    conspiring to laugh despite the dry well
    despite the spell the diviners spoke
    conspiring not to weep
          sunkún
                sunkún sunkún
                        kò sunkún
And the other guard
who did not appreciate their nervous laughter

"We-were-one-of-many-who-left"
"The-wave-returns-but-
  departs-differently"
"How-many-
  times-
  has-this-story-been-told"
These were the names
the ones who cast divination
when immigration first occurred
when we were first cast
when a star smaller than hope
flashed due north
The story
returns

INCANTATION BEFORE DEPARTURE

The hermit crab can be heard carrying his home
discarded leaves provide an orchestra for the traveler—
the sound of immigration changes quickly
        in children—
This was the song the griot gestured
words bouncing off hollowed trunks of almond tree, ackee tree,
      breadfruit
slings of goatskin gesturing tones on drums
(on the day we went in search of flora
      the day we washed words
      turning them to incantations
      clean & sharp like the edge of leaves—
The day we recorded a new road
      upon the atlas of memory)

Before leaving they needed to verify if the story would continue
if the flora would mirror the other
back home
        or
    flowered
        another shape
if they would see themselves as before
      although:
The accents blend with the noise
The colors se ensaladan
The salad is called something else
The rhythm resides deeper, at other intervals, harder to access

They said to atone with volumes of story
some cooled the cracking ground by recalling the atlas of their
journeys
      The mouth now moist like that of wise fish

The hermit crab can be heard carrying his home
traveling through the orchestra of fallen leaves—
The language of immigration changes quickly in children—

Rio Nuevo, Jamaica

BEFORE BECOMING WISE FISH

Who would suffer if you looked
          into the mirrored sea
    so long
    yr head saw illusion
    so long
    the sacred was deluded by waves
    so long
    because migration begins with a lap 'n' a flip
          away from the source . . .

You oar even more
    waves grow
        teeth threat
        soak our hymns our
        plumed language
          like heavy rain on pelican's wing
    But slowly
        memory of bembé y bàtá
        the procession de Yemọjá
          disguised as La Virgen de Regla
            on September
            7th
            on her way to that
              bay—
        slowly
          waves foam our memory
            like froth on her feet

Arturo reached the edge de la bahía
cast cuatro lobes of coconut
just beyond reach of waves:
    dice que "Ọ̀kànràn"
one with white mouth opened skyward

the other three splattered facedown—
that many criollitos
    se escaparán
in boats floating like
    looking like
bottles with empty sheets of paper . . .

BRINCANDO EL CHARCO
(THIS IS CALLED COURAGE)

I.

If all these fish paddled to this shore
and it was time to leave
and you poured a small bottle of molasses
and the stones summoned there
drank it
and a floating coco
smiled into four lobes
their pulp pointing favorably
and they flirted with a wave
and eventually kissed yr feet
If on Friday the twenty-fourth you snuck into un monte
and spilled to yr left yr right
small balls of cornmeal
and heard certain whistles
but stayed on yr trail
and you found a certain forge
draped with palm fronds
and the water was still dancing
to an odd kín-ki-láck   ká-ká-gùn   kín-ki-láck   ká-ká-gùn
and you splashed yr last bath
(because it was time to leave)

If this can be birth of courage
If leaving the known for the unknown
If jumping the big puddle
If they said you will not return for some time
If you can resist forgetting
If the waves will wipe yr memory
If yr children will reject yr lengua of heat of
      jungle of

tún-ro-ko-tún of
gypsy wails of
spirits of . . . of . . . of . . .
but you look at esos cocos kissing yr feet
and you believe the story will continue
and it'll be a while before it's told

II.

Who smithies an idea
then casts its form unto story
song of iron song of conflict
Who has the courage to listen to
   the clank of imagination to
   create the columns that spread the bridge to
   weld bilingual links to
   bold a new image with eyes so bloodshot
      honoring the before
Who fearless would own those eyes

Whose image we sculpt as a pile of iron
Who drinks mucho aguardiente
Who smokes mucho tabaco
Who dances with a skirt of máríwò
Who bathes in palm oil & 7 herbs including mókogún
Who clears a dense path with a green 'n' black cutlass

Who is aboriginal of arrival on this side
Who must chisel a survival acting alone
Who still petitions Òrìshà, Loa, Vodún, Nganga
Who cannot forget what came before
Who alters the invisible by blending herbs
  by spraying words
  unto the scene

Who mails money medicine hand-me-downs
     to the sister living near a vacant plaza
Who is aboriginal of arrival
Who must chisel a survival
     acting alone
This is called courage
Brincando el charco
Who . . . who . . . who . . .
Tótó hun . . .   Hun-hun

VEVE / FIRMA

Someone
(they can be dressed in white linen) goes
gets into the head of rhythm
spills lime chalk in small curls & arrows
chalk we call ẹfun
cascarilla también
spills it for specific purpose—
we call this veve
firma también
también gandó

In order to summon Loa
Òrìshà maybe
maybe Nganga
the signature must seem like mirror
visual dance at the door to the earth
like a replay of the past
conflict & tears
immigrant who first
steps on foreign soil acting
alone
opening a path through el monte
The one who arrives with red eyes
machete y máríwò
smithies courage
then slices bits to his children

The signature must seem like
mirror like iron thread
from this world to
that world

BACK HOME A SPLASH CAN
ONLY COME FROM A FISH

Far from here
from this portal in el Caribe
there is a river where my mother
                    sprung from
The stones assembled like stairs
grooves where she placed her combs of coral
cradled her people's hopes
grooves formed by the softness of her water

People say they've seen flashes of small shadowy fish
with red feathers for dorsals—
they undulate
greeting those who gather on
the bank with brass bells
gourds of honey
fresh ferns lettuce
feathers spread like a fan
splashing ineffable droplets
as only wise fish can do—

They said to perform this ceremony back home
with a red African Grey feather on your head—
you will remember the countless miles traveled
stories only wise fish can tell

THE BIRTH OF AN ABIKÚ

I.

Many women did this then
    (at the birth of an abikú)
The one who sang with a drum of metaphors
        rich & melodic
that hovers like a noon sun of verbal beats
announced the child's arrival
with the words of Èjì Ẹ́lẹ́mèrè
The child
    born feetfirst
        with a faint layer of sand
This child
    did he come by way of ocean
        from el río
            a stray desert back home
            from a certain ancestor who drowned in high seas?

But they saw Èjì Ẹ́lẹ́mèrè
they said he was staying temporarily
The child still had his caul wrapped around his shoulder
    white & dingy display of innocence
when they introduced him to the earth
to the sculptured wooden tray
& its four directions
They whispered into his ear
    "Salakó, Salakó"
He responded porque this was his actual name
hidden & subtle
(Salakó meaning spread the white cloth)
And there was the indelible mark—
the missing piece of earlobe
His history was known
the abikú's history

These women
their hair plaited peculiar
in braids that apexed into a crown
They collected escoba amarga y espanta muerto
The small sour flowers would whip
the ancestral memory of departure
the child's return to the other world
the temptation of desertion

There was the wooden doll
chiseled from ceiba, quiebra hacha, cedar, or laurel, or yaya
This doll would represent
the breath the infant left behind
the ancestral shadow
witness of all his secrets
the jealous twin who at any moment could
call on his brother to return—
the doll was to prevent this

These women summoned those prolific leaves
summoned powdered eggshells & lime chalk
        the ashes of palo moruro
the necessary cloth
that would cover the newborn skin
the small chain with brass bell
The Awó who sang the odù
with history in his heart
fastened the child to the earth
draped him with dangling rags with old signatures
    (the writing was done with ashes & powders)
Done was the task of birth & departure &
        rebirth
Done was the shattered joy of infant death

the constant concern of the fruit of dreams
cascading
the unforeseen fall from a barbacoa
Done was the frustration of drawing water
                with a tattered basket

The old signatures sent messages in a resonant tone
a tattoo into space
much like the Abeng
those Caribbean conch blowers
who notified the breeze of their freedom

In the surrounding cane fields & barracones built
                with sweet mud of molasses
yet another child grows & learns this same art
In 25 years he does the same as they did to him
to another version of the poet who fastened him—
in 25 years he does the same as they did to him

II.

There seems to be no way around this—
They arrive with their multicolored grins
unsure of the geomusical dynamics
They chisel their island
dream it with sweat
They leave tracks of salt on the roadside—
sculptures
drums & horns
some with grooves swaying clearly
Ports
sunken with activity
crates
strewn wheels spawned gardens

overgrown graveyards
all telling an unfinished tale of birth & sudden death
because a planned exile would've ritualized their memories
Evidence of ceremony would be obvious

But why the sudden departure—
was it the silencing of voices
or was it that no one recorded the previous stories
the cautious tale
or was it that the same hole was waiting
At one point
only a man & three women
witnessed the event
The man fell into a hole
until he was rescued with the thrice-joined head-tie

The sole surviving shrill
that sung with history in its heart
& love on its tongue

III.

Near the sanctioned parks
a naked jungle's imitation
near the stuccoed structures & glass-blown markets
yet another child grows & learns this same art
In 25 years he does the same as they did to him—
in another home
pioneer of another geomusical groove
He grew & learned the same art
the hermetic dance of words
to do the same as they did to him
(same as they did to him)

CUCHILLO DE DOBLE FILO (I)

This can be amulet
against conflict—
a machete the size of wind
to cut through guerra between us—
because you
speak Spanish
me parle Creole—
Machete the size of wind
to cut through conflict

Seven ropes with iron links
descended
gave us their hands
like a good friend—
this is how we pull the creative spirit
bit by bit
how we pull the machete
the size of wind
to remove the conflict

       *

There were many who left
we left many behind—
tía hermano y abuela
many left behind—
in Jacmel Cap-Haitien
Ti Jean who often offered songs of rara
all he ever had
who often didn't eat
who was arrested often
Tío Juan who often offered una yambú
all he ever had
en a sad corner de tristeza
because many were hungry often

who often didn't eat
who were arrested often

We have assembled on the sandy edge of Port-au-Prince
of Varadero
        Come & see
There were many who left petitions to Ò. gún
(Panamá, Ferraille/Yorùbá, Alágbedè)
displayed on desolate railroad track
to give them a machete
to clear the path to another land
Miami perhaps
But no one asked how sharp
the blade was going to be
how double-edged
it was to be
cuchillo de doble filo—
(Ikírí adá Ò. gún l'obe Ò. gún lo pa l'obe)

We have assembled on the sandy edge of Miami
come & see—
There were many left behind
Come & see the empty rafts
Come
Come & see the empty boats
Come & see we
boat people

UN REZO TO RECONCILE

I.

There are periods
long periods at a time when you consider
how to reconcile the ocean
& the moon—
she with her mantle of indigo
spread easily
favorable to invisible flow
host of shipwrecks
tomb to many a human cargo
witness to vast immigrations
vast enough to host
there are rainbows who've lost their way

She with her silver breath
spread easily
every breath dancing like waves
favorable to slow flow of ellipses
conspirator to shipwrecks
who gave them the terminal wink
lit candles at the tomb of human cargo
witness to vast immigrations
vast enough when
there are stars who've lost their way

II.

You can sit cross-legged & contort yr lips & praise
distances
but the writings on the yellow sand
say differently—
they speak of a silent smile that's attached to the earth
still & content

Hay immigrants lining the shore strewn
like burnt seaweed
waves who push them further
inland
away from their source
And there are some who will forget
the kiss from that wave
And there are some who return to settle there—
en el canto se encuentran
Hay lovers standing on a bridge
they meet to say things they interpret from destiny's mouth
they kiss & make horrible gestures &
grow old together
And there are wise fish who circle the bridge
they hear fumbled memories
witness new arrivals
cloaked in a mantle of indigo
hands stained by silver breath
they huddle to send smoke signals to whoever will listen

There are periods
long periods at a time when you . . .

en el canto se encuentran

THE SOUND OF ONE IMMIGRANT CLAPPING

—after Czeslaw Milosz

Let's say he actually
did not
arrive on a boat—
that the relentless colonel
never found his subtle throat hidden
under the trance of the clave
or thunder hands that spoke
repiques of those crimes
Let's say he went to Nueva York
on the assumption
Mario Bauzá
Machito or
Tito (Rodríguez or Puente)
could make his legs & hips move
in a constellation of joy
Let's say he merely
tried
to hear the echo of his arms
flapping through a factory
like a red rag fastened to that fan
Let's say the cold
often froze his vowels
tan Caribeña
tan resbalosa y mermelada—
Could the immigrant even
mute the melody of his tongue—
They say it is silence
that makes music

But this will be like
drumming
on a distant tuft of cloud like
the colonel cutting the sound he never found
But it takes years of forgetting
for a stranger
to breathe the saltwater
or glance at a pile of stones
& say
I arrived through this portal
This is now my home . . .

BOMBILLO EVER AFTER

—*for the memory of Felix Gonzalez-Torres*

Se te encendió el bombillo
when the image was strung
with illumined idea
like those old twilights in La Habana
which were slowly erased by the procession of lights
                    woven
                            between homes
strung with illumined idea
            like lazy flea market
            flickering around SoHo

There's a string of little stars
glimpses into the soft elimination of darkness
                    spirit-like
suspended as if by accident
as if this room's evening
        were eclipsed by
            yr dialogue with death
        the whole question of epilogue—
            if little stars dim

You who thought Dios/Olórun
an excuse for the admittance of misery
I love the irony of yr death—
when bombillo blows
it happens without mercy

swift & obvious
                    so
continual
inconsequential
Ya tú lo sabes

You who arrived in Nueva York
armed with yr concepts & ideas
y fueron los bombillos
that lit yr work
se fueron los bombillos
that were most impressive
that reminded you of yr childhood home
barrio y callejón

You who thought God/Olórun
an excuse for fatalism
I love the irony of yr death—
so long as someone's eye
se enciende with the hope of América
yr debate will continue
with yr people
with yr death
if little stars dim or
el bombillo lit
ever after

HONEYMOON IN CHINA

—*for Siu*

She might've loved the island
after all
she wore her white uniform of love
the first & last time
there—
she wore her white uniform a long way for the honeymoon
China can be far from El Barrio Chino
Beijing with its big wall of incense & qi
Shaolin temples
herbalists with prescriptions from previous dynasties
martial artists who
dedicated their lives to singing
the body divine
were not bereft of expression
yet

They went to China on a honeymoon
but displays of gunpowder
the blood running forming puddles
on dirt roadsides
soon kept them in the largest of prisons
And after 63 years
several children
after much sorrow & laughter
exile & remembering
she would never see la bodega en El Barrio Chino
where she opened a door
to another home
where she met her destiny
to another life

THE MYSTERIES COME TO THE BRIDGE

—for Edouard Duval Carrié

The mysteries come to the bridge
The embarkation can be Haitian
    itself a basket of fruits
      forced to float from Ibo, Yorùbá, Kongo
        Dahomey country
The embarkation can be Cuban too
    itself a canasta of fruits
    the mysteries come al song
            de tambores bàtá

There are fish who kiss this boat
they too are wise because they witness & remember
Òshun quien es Ezuli
Ògún es Ogu (aqui viene Ògún, Ògún, Ògún)
Loko es Iroko
    Iroko/Loko (kó kò kó)
Legba/Elegba, Èshù Òdàrà
    who delivers messages with a morse code of offerings
Dambala coiled in a snake of white cloth
      Obatálà y/o Nana Burukú
Yemojá/Olókun
    Olókun/Agwe
hosting the onslaught of oars
on their soft tablecloth of blue
Òrúnmìlà slowly sang the journey—Ifá

They departed like a whispered incantation
    the shore was assisted by
      sea grapes, which we call uvi de caleta
      by lengua de vaca
      by albahaca
And there were crabs y carey

turtles who teared only an antenna
        only an eye
while the other bid farewell
It was quiet

This story is repetitious
Their boat was made of calabash—
                they sliced the upper world & this world
                they used the upper to cover their heads
                the lower to dance on water
                There were certain signatures
                        incantations etched
                        there were smaller gourds dangling on the sides
                        some beaded some painted
                History has it they were packed with juju
                        the ancestor of mojo
                        le dicen brujería
                        le dicen nishe Òsàyìn

When the embarkation arrived
        smooth like fingers sliding through powder
they saw a similar scene
The flora smiled
        like an old friend:
        Botón de oro spilled a golden button
        Pèrègún with its bayonet provided defense
        Campanas rung their silent scent
        And there was Ceiba
            Iroko's brother who they called
                            Àràbà
                —it too had a white cloth circling its trunk—
The mysteries smiled
        Tradition migrated

When the embarkation arrived
only the names had changed
names changed
like yours
like mine

INCANTATION FOR THE WORD

Shi-shi   shah-shah   shi   she-eeh
is the music of divination powder
Takatakatakataka
is the music of palm nuts conversing/(ikin)
Ikin can
speak of a certain matter burrowed in sand
Odù is the music of
Ọmọlú is the music of
                that speech

And we arrived with these pronouncements
circling a wooden tray
circling those signatures (who summon the true name of
things)
like coded messages from birds soaked
with the dew of universe
archetypes & all
past present & therefore
                future
many languages with rhythm & all
even tonal
circling a wooden tray
tray who circular implies
          WORLD
And it is word who causes this dance
And there are rhythmic leaps into
the sweetness of abundance into
the iron crest of creativity
And there herbs who cause the invisible to manifest
And it is word who causes this dance
Takatakatakataka
is the music of palm nuts conversing/(ikin)
Yes we can initiate a dialogue between known &

unknown
between those who flow round jagged stones of ignorance
river-like
like wise fish
we can bring messages regarding history
the ineffable speech of music
the music of verse
vibration from spirits through ripples
rhythm residing deep among the lushness
An old beaded crown invokes the power of poem
—in an incantation we can

Odù is the music of
Ọmọlú is the music of
                that speech
  Shi-shi   shah-shah   shi   she-eeh
                shshsh!

THE TRANCE/MIGRATION OF SOUND

White cloth like caul spread
in the midst of motion
meanderings like crisp conga solos
pools of wisdom dancing
now & again
—motion of river & a simple
thought—
we are born of rhythm
sound simply migrates & mixes

      (Milt Jackson hovering over
          vibes
    now & again glancing up at
          spirits
           to check
      if they still snapping
         in 3/4 time
         if they still
         with him
         (ancient
   balafon man
   still spiritized
   still oracular
after all these African
    ballads spoken
    American
balafon man)—

In the midst of motion
currents curving like crisp conga solos
pools of wisdom churning
          rising changing
          history with all his apologies
          chatting alone

There will be 3 boats arriving soon
they come with cooperation of wave & wind
salt will eat the helm soon
soon el capitán will denounce the waves as traitors
—it was his nature—
soon the nature of
necessity
to unload many crates of bacalao
when it gave an itching
          salty scratching sweating
          creativity with all her invasions
          conquering totally
Soon they gathered these cajónes—
     they began to klá-klò—
     while another said um-im-om
     while hands were slow
     the air was laced with heat
     & there were three boats—

They called it Yambú
the one que no se vacuna
          pools of wisdom churning
          rising changing
          history with all his apologies
          rhythm de Africa
          Spanish bacalao
          speech de un babalawo
          Afro en América
          dancing at a crossroad
          en Miami

Vacuna: action when a man & woman mimic
          the courts of ancient rooster & hen
               ay dios!
               (ay dios!)
               ((aaayyy!))
          Strutting courting
          strutting mixing churning
          history with all his apologies—

               changing

ONE IRONY OF THE CARIBBEAN

It is common knowledge:
these waters witnessed the meet between East & West

Those sullen sailors rancid with chorizo
talcumed with salt & sea breeze
old gunpowder
the perennial scent of Spain flapping
               among the crested flags
the debauched night of laud
    the Moorish cumin
        the Gypsy's dervish

But Tainos had mango o guanábana
to hoist as flag
perhaps a carey & tabaco leaf as insignia
They used planks from siguaraya
o quiebra hacha
pine or cedar
(that perfumed at the same time)
while sailing to the Areyto plaza
And the Caribs
well they used bones with hatchet scars
for mere decoration
in effect a floating coffin

The triangle that ensnared freedom
corralled continents into a trinity of suffering
the ships which chiseled these shores
in effect floating coffins

They departed from these islands
in rafts at best
hammered & fastened from rafters

from dangling colonial homes
in Regla, Cojimar, Marianao,
Jacmel Cap-Haitien
the same homes built
by survivors of floating coffins
They built them
with the same wood that bolted their ancestors' chains
The same wood glued with sugarcane sap
They used strewn army canvases for sails
the sails that pivoted
often in the wrong direction
A rudder fashioned from a shovel
stained with the earth of a dead man
They launched it to sea
to begin anew
but in effect a floating coffin

A long time ago
they didn't bury the dead
till the eyes were pecked by a mysterious bird
delivered to the heavens
so the eyes could oversee the body's proper burial
It was then that
they buried the body
in a hollowed trunk of siguaraya,
quiebra hacha, pine, or cedar
sometimes ceiba for chiefs & priests
They launched it to sea to reach home to
reunite with the others
they lauched it to sea
to begin anew
in effect a floating coffin

PARA LA INSTALLATION DE JOSÉ BEDIA

Que tu son Kongo
emi ni son Yorùbá
canto en Inglés—

The marriage of spirit & history
is often like a dance of streams
dance of rainbows
like sending smoke signals yes there is
                    hope
& yes we can resist the urge to forget

The brick boat
with its shadow about to speak
tells the story
So we gather bits of myth—
something like balsas
something like torn cloth
armed with little war instruments
Shovel & hoe to erect roots
(they can be amuletos so long you keep them in yr pocket
necklace yr head)
Something like rope
like white head-tie
to provoke stability & peace of mind
Something like strewn slipper de niño
we call this chancleta
we call this sorrow

Que tu son Kongo
emi ni son Yorùbá
canto en Español—

E yo hala garabato mi Kongo
mi Kongo
Kongo real
hala garabato halo

We who are born from river water
seawater
tambor y trueno
repique de brisas & stones
We who circle clouds of cotton
with a certain chant
We who choose el canto—
in Spanish or Kongo Biriyumba
Òshà Lukumí
Monina Nkama
in Arará kwero Dahomey e e
We who build shrines to migration
We who die with
river water seawater
tambor y trueno
repique de brisas & stones

Those who cast the first balsa
in the bombardment of boats
who cast a desperate wail
Pablo, Antonio, Miguel
maybe even Raquel
They said one throws the rock
but it's the people who get blamed
it's the people who get blamed
when one throws the rock
(Oye basta de cuento
llego el momento de—)

Those who cast the first balsa
even though they've seen empty
even bitten inner tubes
lying softly on a breezy shore
even though they've seen the iron rudder
with the signature of Sarabanda Kimbansa
strewn on a pile of stones
strewn like dead fish

*

He who struts con crutches
but dances without them
has a body of trembles
but inside has signs of infinity—
a dog can be his messenger

San Lao San Lao
Kobayende San Lao

He who sits at crossroads
changing destinies with a funny dance
sometimes from pebble to sugar
from sugar to pebble

*

Que tu son Kongo
emi ni son Yorùbá
canto en Lukumí—

Èshù òdàrà ibà re o
Òrúnmìlà kò soro odà ni òfò

kò soro òfò ni odà
Ifá ri o
Adashe
Four twins spin a hymn—
something about opening yr eyes
to what is before you
(Irosùn méjì)
about being led into a trap
(Irosùn méjì)
They said no one knows what's at the bottom of the sea
They said you must be careful
There's someone with big boots
standing on a shore
& yes there's a hole just ahead
You must be careful
the ocean seems to be hungry these days—

A NEW ATLAS

Ti-ting will always follow tu-tún
    in the bellows of hymns
        if our rhythm is to continue—
    when we flap with a lip & a flip
        (away from the source)

    not only Flamenco corners
    not only Areito plazas
    not only Asere Ekpe Muñongo Efo
    not only Iyálode alade oyin
        crown of honey
    but the chatter of hands
    but the toss of piropos
    but the bustle of waves
    & the splash of voices
        tán-tán
            criollo

Ti-ting will always follow tu-tún
in the cauldron of rhythms—
we begin to blend impressions
tú con Cubano
we with Boriqua
Afro con América
Santo con Domingo
They said
    some ma-machete could clear routes
        could root
            a new identity strung
                with bilingual links of iron
they said
    pour a pint of palm oil
        slaughter a bottle of aguardiente

spray a black rooster above the links
they said
       even the machete también
       would have to dance también
       sharp & slippery

Ti-ting will always follow tu-tún
we forge incantations
               tones
                       laced with the history of monte adentro—
                       the jungle becomes our cohort
                                   through these hymns
                               through these hymns
                       we remove fallen trunks
                           like lifting hollow figs
                           like this has secretly been the method
Three gourds plunge from their source
each speak with a slight nasal whistle:
       Oye camina muchacho un poco ma' pa' lante
       you'll find ese river
       rio that has the root
       the thought like water
       oracle to spill
                           it
               herb to spiritize
                       it
               stone to memorize
                           it
Welcome to the home of wise fish—
Who
       will read the wet letter writ with cowries
who
       will chant the links of the traditions?

FISHING AT THE CROSSROADS

"hablo de la ciudad construida por los muertos, habitada por sus tercos
   fantasmas, regida por su despótica memoria,
la ciudad con la que hablo cuando no hablo con nadie y ahora me
   dicta estas palabras insomnes"
—OCTAVIO PAZ

If we begin anywhere it would be here, where crossing destinies
   meet & call it home,
near the ocean, lakeside, railroad tracks, a spring in someone's
   backyard, a baseball field sequestered by an intercoastal,
   Cuban cafeterias serving pit stops of café, tabacos Padron y
   Maribel,
near the river of grass where they once canoed dodging mosqui-
   tos with precise missions, water moccasins wearing a ring
   of glory, some wanted to trade catfish & alligator skins but
   now mostly want to be left alone to celebrate on a ham-
   mock,
near the lonely corner of her dream, the market that sold mem-
   ories, the big city enclosed in a bedroom, quiet like sunrise,
near her body lying near, shiny like the crackle of sun peeking
   its head from the edge of ocean,
near the two gumbo-limbo trees where she hung her ham-
   mock, simple engineering that sprung a family name,
near the guanábana, mango, mamey, papaya, aguacate, tomato,
   tamarindo, flowers growing into fruits, seeds abandoned by
   birds commissioned to wind, to distribute strawberry pep-
   pers, ají cachucha, chile, key limes, naranja ágria, SUNSHINE
   ORANGES,
where the air is pregnant with droplets, sticky, ready to embrace
   everyone, thicker at night, bamboo leaves wrestle angrily,
near parrots who escaped their caged jungle in August 1992, who
   cackle a strange gossip, they're never lonely, even when
   asleep, you see them in mobs of green & blue clouds
   announcing their arrival,

near the three days of winter when you hear planes departing,
   the rumble of destination, late night, the crackle of night—

If we begin anywhere it would be here, east to west on Calle
   Ocho putas parade with perennia confidence, open for late
   lunch, motels flicker "MOVIES," the residue of exhaust coats
   the fierce flora on the roadside black, the lawn of marble
   awaits across the street, the moist soil, the granite moss,
near where carnivals spring forth, they love Celia, Tito, Oscar,
   Andy, & Rubén, because what happens happens, the music
   is good, & she finally dances with him, & it's Sunday, y
   mañana todo el mundo a trabajar,
near the crowded hills of paper plates, cups, improvised fans,
   teenage love letters, photos, break-ups, reunions, first
   kisses, honeymoons, the world's largest conga-line herds
   through here, 500,000 people whose feet show their history,
near parks with immortal flames dancing before a ceiba, its
   roots bigger than tyrants, hopeful heroes, its roots a grave-
   yard of sacrifices, the immortal flame where they gather to
   denounce, tremble their aging fists of frustration,
where they arrive in waves of hope, often saved by Coast
   Guards, some who hobble into lush lobbies, guessing their
   location by the maids' faces, in the spirit of Crusoe, they
   whisper, "no es fácil, no es fácil," then the other one says it
   again,
where they sleep tonight, when the cameras have closed their
   eyes & memorized as always their desperate statements,
where the uncle, brother, cousin, mother, lover, wife, watched
   astonished on the nightly news,
where they have hidden the last 25,000, the last 120,000, the last
   97,000, or so, when they send them back, where do they
   hide? when they try again, on a bigger boat, cargo stow-
   away, the lucky airplane whose propeller sings forever

sweet, when the welcome is sadder than the betrayed, spo-
ken, secret departure,
where the conspiracy of languages bounces off heads like radio
signals, people here have antennas sensitive to accents,
everyone has at least one,
where elements from one mix to become moros y congrí,
ajiaco, patacón y tostón, tamal y pastel, bollitos y akarajé,
okra/quimbombó/molondrón,
where Dominican marries Cuban, & Cuban Jamaican, Jamaican
marries Colombian, & Colombian Haitian, Haitian marries
Brazilian, & Brazilian Boricua, Miami is us, unidos thus,
near neighbors scattered like spots on leopards who come & go
from the spirit world by uttering certain words, archaic
African words, they drift temporarily, listen, nod, then
bring back the message, pull it from a pocket magically,
babalawos cast brass chain with 8 lobes of coconut shell, sil-
ver, or ivory, they interpret certain poems & proverbs, they
often chant them in antique tones, they write to those
who can't write what has not been written for those who
can't write, by doing so they send a vibration that alters
the invisible, like the quantum stone thrown here causing
a typhoon in Thailand, they blend herbs & snaps from the
natural world, figments of incantations, make them dance
with their mystical songs, la ciudad bruja, la vida bruja,
across the street tambores TÚN: they often have a bembé,
toque de santo, bàtá drums like up thus:

       okonkolú   Iyá Ilú   Itotélè

they send telegrams to the citizens of the other world in a
tonal tongue, the KÁ-KÙN-KÙN-KÙN-KÍ KA-KÍ-KÍ-KÍ KA-KÚN, KA-KÚN,
KÀ, coats your plexus with globs of honey, your lips lap up
the sweetened sound like a hungry fish,

across the street tambores TÚN: KUKUNDÉ, KUKUNDU KÙKÙNDÙNKÙN,
   the red rooster with the proud, long, black feather courts
   the marble painted hen café con leche, KUM-A-KIN, they tell
   stories in clave, the rhythmic pattern of our history,
   Cuban blues/guaguancó, the history of Spain's marriage to
   Africa, the pains of these children, otherwise called timba,
   as in, Tito's got timba, as in troubadours with timba

If we begin anywhere it would be here,
near the cavern-like ficus we call jaguey, there's a plate with fish
   bathed in palm oil, three balls of cornmeal & fried frijoles,
   which no one eats but the invisible, in the shade people
   huddle like vultures, wobble pigeon-like, the neighbor
   who deposits bits of hope at the crossroads, today she will
   disperse her troubles like the intersecting arrows she draws
   on the earth, she leaves nine pennies, a bag wrapped like a
   coffin, & rainbows of candy, while Julio begins, el Niño
   ends, hurricanes begin, & some are defeated, laughed at,
   yet they all return, it is in their nature to be nurtured &
   devoured, crowned & tricked,
Near the empty plate of food at the feet of the ficus, the crossroads
   crack with the sparkle of hope that makes América thus—

CUCHILLO DE DOBLE FILO (II)

There were many who were left
we left many behind
There
they will continue
the traditions of walking to the pulse of papayas
the language their children will continue
they will carry on
the smooth Caribbean relax
Here
there are many who will forget
who will cut the root con un cuchillo
de doble filo

We summon 7 ropes with iron links
to give us a hand
like an old friend
We fasten the links to their memory
We say the hunter always carries his bow—

There were many who were left behind—
Come & see the empty rafts
Come
Come & see the empty boats
come & see we
boat people

WHEN SHE CARRIED A CALABASH

—for Katherine Dunham

They said the calm calabash will spill
I say the calm calabash will spill

There was no particular destination
these vines crawled
generously
defying gravity up
the textured wall up
la mata de paraíso
magically opening a venous path
curled like a juju-man's caduceus
un bastón de Babalawo
Ifá ni Èròmásunká— Hiinn
Mo ni Èròmásunká— Hiinn

Subtle
hammocked below dense leaves
propped proudly
the amber calabash
(Not so many know
it was used to house the first lantern—
she packed it with nutmeg & myrrh
the herbs of maravilla & marilope
orozus romerillo rosemary
red palm oil spilled for fuel
She lit the path to the river
when they traveled from island to island
thirsty
Down the Tamiami Canal
she carried the calabash down Calle Ocho
beginning en los Everglades
balanced between braids & brass beads

she embraced with both hands
down the coral-lined trench
the muddy gun range
the erratic awkwardly placed sprawl
the concrete overpass
down the storefronts
the successive botánicas
the nostalgic cafés
with the thick ting of Chapotín's trumpet
snuggled by fertile matas de coco
she danced wave-like down NE 2nd Avenue
diggin' the golden brown murals of the
days when boogie-woogie & big-band proclaimed the actual
story
like Melton with the crescent embouchure
Through Wynwood
still on NE 2nd
todo el mundo swiveling hips
frying bacalaitos
waves of abichuelas blooped
al son de Tito's timbal
Giovanni's secret hand
Eddy Gua-gua's cruise down baby bass harmony
When she carried a calabash in Buena Vista
only her name changed
Erzuli po' mago
they said through the clewon
the Rara drums walking thick on Bolu's hands
a constant tick-tock of skins jockeying
the echo of Morriseau-Leroi's exiled creolizations
bouncing through the mystical market of language
Ifá ni Èròmásunká— Hiinn
Mo ni Èròmásunká— Hiinn

And this here is an incantation
a wave arising from breath into sound into word
a wave altering the invisible like
when lovers kiss below a flowering canopy
Ifá ni Èròmásunká— Hiinn
Mo ni Èròmásunká— Hiinn

Now turning her way back home
she carried a calabash back home
down to the Oletta River
She stopped for the children of Abeng
those Jamaican conch blowers
who notified fish
wise fish of freedom
in an ancient tone she knew—
everyone was home
now
She collected some of our objects of sound
In the end
laced them side by side ensnaring them
In the end—
a net circling the calabash that when shaken
would sound of a call—
Ifá ni Èròmásunká Hiinn
Mo ni Èròmásunká— Hiinn

They said the calm calabash will spill
I say the calm calabash will spill

Mother's Day, 1999

REGARDING IRON

during divination

"When-one's-strength-has-subsided
we-spray-aguardiente-by-the-door"
"Iron-does-not-yield-to-palm-frond"—
were the ones who cast cowries
for the owner of iron (Alágbedè)
were the ones who spoke of its uses
when Ògún's child was first formed
when he arrived in foreign land
when he wandered what to do
with his father's legacy
his father's relic

They said *epo mà l'èrò epo mà l'èrò*
        Ajala epo mà l'èrò
They said iron must be bathed in palm oil
so it may scissor with an easy ting
across uncarved images
across the chorus of silence
They said con corojo, con corojo

And don't forget the cacophony of iron's kiss
They said he could use its strength como clave
to keep rhythm in order
they said to call his father often
Ògún can hear the clank of creation
descend through Lukumí helix links
touch the shoulder of the creative
They said with rhythm

Ògún's child kneeled before his father's legacy
his father's relic—
"When-one's-strength-has-subsided

we-spray-aguardiente-by-the-door"
"Iron-does-not-yield-to-palm-frond"—
were the ones who cast cowries
for the owner of iron (Alágbedè)
were the ones who spoke of its uses—
Iron
    who suddenly shapes art
    whose edge clears the creative path
Iron
    whose music tings
    like sharp cackle
    whose head imagines a bridge
    whose feet forge a cane
    whose owner acts alone
Iron
Hierro
Irinnnnnnn

REUNION

Again you've reached that secret nook
that stream where words mix to bond you to me
Or is it the sentimental mood of your voice
maybe the song the moon was beaming
silently almost full
upon a blank page
upon your letters
It could be the void I feel
every night before sleep
that feeling I keep failing to tell you about
every night since you've been gone
Before sleep I turn to feel your skin
your stomach
the skin between your thighs
as I trace your lips with my fingers
but every night you've been gone

But tonight
though the moon will beam almost full
again
alas it will be different
she will shine on yr lips
on mine
when they meet
long before sleep

MISA
CARIBEÑA

FLOWERS, PHOTO, A GLASS
OF WATER FOR OCTAVIO

I just heard the news about
Octavio pájaro de paz con pico de palabra

Last night I was working on the city prose poem
     (serious attempt but immature compared to yours)
I wonder of our timing:
did your last breath escape as I read aloud
     "your hungry city which bears mother-like
   but also devours us"
was it when I wrote
     "where the conspiracy of language bounces off heads . . . "
when I wrote
     "where elements from one mix to become . . . "

It was two years ago to date when we met
under circumstances you
couldn't possibly remember—
there were the multitudes who vibrated
with your just-sung lines
un mestizaje de imagen

Back in '97 they said you also died
yet you proved them follied
But today is not a game
not only because the radio said so
but because my picture of Pablo smiled last night
as if greeting an estranged friend
as I reread "Hablo de la ciudad" so intently

This is a strange & simple connection Octavio
narcissistic
            but you now know nonetheless true
I will place your photo, una flor, & a glass of water next to
Pablo's
between the signature poets use
I just heard the news Octavio
a blanket of goosebumps flood my skin,
my eyes flush with the news of a fallen bird
I pull over
seek shelter from myself
& curl my lower lip

HOODOO WHISPER

—for Quincy Troupe

Say it in sheets of sound
power of language with big fists of teeth
singing secrets from the crossroads
saying secrets from the hoodoo
way up in East St. Louis soil
the groove of alphabets
in the blues of a new atlas
way up in a silent way
like the sho-nuff shaman man you am

Say it because
the pact was sealed in the other world—
There are some
who could claim the word for hisself
who would wrap it in red cloth
could caress it along fire
like the marriage between flame & light
who dip it in a repique of thunder
make yr head flicker with the spirit of rhythm rhythm of spirit
as if Shangó hisself
had weaved you a red kufi

And there are some
who trap the odù way up in them bones
who spill the past & therefore future
between blood & honey
divine what ain't nobody seen
And this here is an oríkí
in praise of the possibility of
ká-ká-ki-ták tún of tongue
in praise of those
claiming their language
tonal y todo
with a hoodoo whisper
like Miles Dewey Davis III
like the sho-nuff shaman man you am
sho-nuff shaman man you am

MISA CARIBEÑA

Verde de ver green were her eyes
where the story began
hidden among almendras
dates, twigs of olive dripping oil

The sting of salt pooling
around ambitious brows
La misa begun by three boats
(rickety in their raucous bouts with breeze)

                    *

                    ¿How to proceed
          when your script has been writ by others
          declared to be in your best interest
          without finding your best interest
                    . . . history
                              with all its difficulties
                              rises from incantation
                              like musk deep
                              in the earth . . .
          —retelling
There's a bundle of bridle memories
          wrapped in white, deep red, then
                    black cloth
strewn like an old photo
                    we turn away from
—retelling
          La liturgia can be bilingual
Latín con Yorùbá
Spanish y Spanish
English con Spanish
Spanish con Latín
Cubano con Yorùbá
someone

61

has to orchestrate this—

El Proceso:
Burn a collection of twigs (Amansa
        Guapo, No-me-olvides, Vencedor, Paramí, Quita Maldición,
        etc. . . .)
Filter to fine dust
Add dried quimbombó
Gather witnesses
Hang the white, red, & black cloth flag-like
Prepare herbal solution for bathing afterwards
Spread ash circular on the ground
Begin writing symbols to span the column from earth to other world
Symbols born from word

There are delicate songs
      that web these worlds
A gourd with salted water
      is awaiting their arrival
When drops pool around fingers
      sliding like rain
          mist of spirits
arrive in chronological death
the sting of salt pooling
      inside our gaping memory
For the future—
we place a table blanketed with pools of cups
fistful of flowers
      candles
here they
      los muertos
can swim
        frolic
After this ash has been etched
we understand how the dead have been received

This is good-bye—
la grande despedida
circled by candles infinite
it can be a signature of sorts
una caja de muerto
the difference is we live
& we continue an odd embrace
                rhythmic

It has been established that
life begins in the ocean
Indeed she who floats on a mantle of blue
sequined with stars & moonlight
is motherhood en persona
& the one chained at the depths who
no one has really seen
collects fragments of bone from
sand
the sound of water choca con hueso
welds the primal bond deep
in the unconscious
Here is where life begins
Here is where
        we
                began
with words on sand
        (close to the tide)
you accepted
I accepted—

A kissed history has dug into the sand
trying to erase the echo of what was writ
You alone gnawing at the mystery
manifested seed-like in my hands
challenging all my efforts

They now have slid off unto
                    otra

I thought though in sand
impermanence would not victimize us
the crystals in your eyes
                    my eyes
sharp & crackling with hope
I thought my feet could shuffle scissor-like slide
                    side to side on sand
printing mysterious messages to you
          (of love, of future, of promise)
I thought the bay pooling around our oath
the reflection of words crystalized there
floating
sinking
delivered with 3 drums bàtá to the origins
I thought they would become sand, then bone
I thought then maybe a child
now I realize
you thought
you thought . . .

                    *

                    ?How to proceed
               when your home itself
                    simple & predictable
               is an abikú—
                         . . . Born transient
                    with scars from previous lives not
                    really indefinite
                    but transient
                    clenching fists of young frustra-
                              tion not
                              yet established
                    alive . . .

                "comb the language"
            with the dorsal from wise fish
            encrusted with coral
                        Filter the rhythm
                        music of
        accents
    "or else"
        end up at the bottom of the sea
        grinding bone con bone
        busy trying to get born
                again
        in another place—

        drops pool from salt
        from fingers sliding like rain
        unto the green
        verde de ver green were her eyes
        where the story begins again
        hidden among almendras

        un llanto gitano se oye
        un llanto gitano dice
    "Que no me lloren
        que no me lloren
        que tengan azucenas
        una guitarra cajón y compás de bulerías
        pañuelos verde y blanco
        que me lloren así"

        This is no secret:
        we are children of death
        Bundled bulky in history
        one white
        deep red

        one black
    textured hymns
ruffled by boats in their raucous breeze
fingering our skin
only a sense
that pools from salt
sand
water
from fingers sliding like rain down skin
unto green verde de ver
            again
            again
            green were her eyes

Misa because there's sand
Misa because there's memory
Misa because there's transformation
Misa because there's fish
because there's ritual
because there's tragedy
Misa because there's music
because there's love
because we mix we survive reborn
Misa porque tú con yo yo con tú
todos mezclados—
Misa caribeña

ÒGÚNDÁ

Ògúndá kara wá Ògún méjè bá kara wá
Òshà dé
Three come cutting through
rants of ignorance
through
the white rooster sadly whistling
he's superior
through
the dog growling at an iron door
to the marketplace selling war
Three come cutting—

They said where we see three
cowries with mouth facing up
among 16 of its siblings
they said we should offer a sacrifice—
this is where Òrìshà shall help conquer the conflict
Ògúndá is like this
(ni jé bé)

There was a time when even
the croa-croa frog frightened the crocodile
If there was a crocodile
who wanted to be owner of the river
If he wanted his destiny to come to pass
what should his questions be—
So he put his hands on his head
when he asked his diviners the path to conquer those conflicts
that will arise
They said he should offer
3 pigeons & 3 bush rats
(this the fuel for courage)

They said offer
palm nut shells
Offer
7 iron pegs
Crocodile heard what needed to be done
In the morning
He met with Elegba on the river bank
If Elegba said
"Open yr mouth"
he fastened iron pegs as teeth
If Elegba said
"Turn on yr belly"
he fastened a layer of shells
on his back
If croa-croa frog came near
Crocodile would clamp his iron teeth
If any fish grazed him
he would slash them with his skin of shells
No one
could frighten
Crocodile
Crocodile became king of the river

And he was dancing like whipping his tail
praising his diviners & Òrìshà
because they had spoken the truth
because his destiny came to pass
Crocodile has his courage
Crocodile has his home . . .

LOISAIDA HAIKUS

Today el sol took
flight con una paloma
the beak of New York

*

The sidewalk takes a
cold shower another day
bereft of tropics

*

Jackhammers sirens
other city music rrrat-
tat-tat fast & shit

*

Celia Tito
Oscar león salsero
in town congas fly

*

Graffiti pigeons
thunder over Loisaida
lyrical breaths bleed

*

The empire was built
bodegas sold Miguel's dreams
rrready to break loose!

*

Guiro y timbal
the streets crackle rhythm
veins highway for arms

*

Boricua you is
You are chewing memory
You of cosmic history

*

Singing the song lifting,
the buildings rise the
gentry keep walking

*

The sky is sad, junk,
puta among the veins
love is now a plague
*
Rats with javelins
frequent trenches of lodo
Even cheese can kill
*
The virgin arrives
flower in her black hair now
a budding puta
*
Pablo the grocer
says free beer on Sunday morn
mouth open with drunks
*
East River aglow
I have reached the end but
there is still no light
*
Avenue D to
Avenue A Nuyori-
can poets healing
*
Born on sidewalk
skin of ink decorations
concrete tribal paint
*
Tomorrow el sol
will wink on a pigeon's eye
culture dreams our breath

New York City, 3/7/92

IN SUMMARY THE AFRICAN CYCLE

A father a son
a brother a son
  A red & black thread
  webs them silently
    until the text is painted
    at first on fine sand
      fresh fingers eager
      to tell the story
        There are others gathered on carved stools
        they too have shared this experience
      Gathered among young gourds
      each with ingredients that shape the roadside subtly
    But the text changes—
    in diagram in image
  in the telling of the text
New characters emerge
to escort the older ones
  to assist in its destined course
  Another branch spiraling outward
    unto the arch of history
    deep into what is known as home
      the memory sold thru generations
      crossing oceans
        It acquires its breath
        finally its breath
          They make in total
          a family of text
        finally a home
        a family as source to spiral from
      until the quiet message
      is writ on ash of various barks
    & you're hoisted out canoe-like
    thru the door you first entered
  to begin anew

HISTORY OF AN ABIKÚ

There are old pictures caressing the table
several marriages between snapshots of the natural world—
    the crocodile's tooth that chewed the ignorant fish
    powdered seeds powdered sticks
    stones marbled with jade & opal
    cowry shells, coral
    certain palm nuts with little eyes
    three, four, & five
    a sculptured container with a head for a lid
        a dome-shaped head
Maybe that is all—
and the burning text that unfolded alongside you
like leaves commissioned to a gust

The message you spread—
at times you carried a brass scepter with a little man seated atop
pointing
a chameleon inching his way upward—
Those changing oaths declaring the power of invocation
the testimonial scars sealed around your mouth
those changing oaths
the changing constructs
The message you spread
like the paroxysmal wave on the sand
that often seemed like ceniza
the residue of a big burned offering
The message you spread
translated
recorded
developed
learned by your heirs
At best
they repeat it
at best
that is all

MISSING ANGELS

When they descended on waxed wings
on our white, our red, brown
on our elevated wings—
is it possible they stole you from
when they ruffled the myriad brushes
that paint our landscape
painted on rhythmic pulse of travel—
Is it possible to wash blood off skin
& flowers off skin

The memory of you my brother
paving the stone trail with soft music
a wandering tumble down our veins
a shift in atlas
the quest for the perennial record
the memory of you
still
archival
like the fact everyone is first from somewhere else

Remember we too migrated—
we once left our signatures on the sand
& on night
sliding through our fingers
like hourglass
And the memory of you
swearing an oath on a steel spike
then offering it deep to the earth & ocean
dead fish looking on

We promised we would not end like the others
forgetful of breeze
the smooth Caribbean relax
of conversation
the humanity of doing nothing

Soon you'll have to answer to the sand you swore
& the steel you swore
because it's possible they've hidden you
buried the script of you
the arching target of history: Yet
blood reaches home soon
Sand will eventually turn to bone
Wind will feel its flesh
Steel will give it body

& there is still music
more music
memorized in stone

CROSS THE WATER

. . . a film score in verse . . .

What it was what she saw spotted
        prancing
            able to pounce
        among the lushness
        cascading trails trenching newly
            crossed water
in those days
    far before oyibo traded palm oil for salt
        gunpowder for slaves
before Asibong Ekondo erected ebony totem over red earth at
Obutong
its friction echoed a guttural speech
        Neneké
In those days Neneké
spotted majestic motion
paws with rings of raffia
& neck with rings of raffia
tail ringing a sonorous call like
        nkaniká
            enticing fish to come & play
bell which oriented dispersed ones
        across water

When Ekpe dances at Uságare
she ripples across the bank
above Cross River
meandering like veins on young paws
                weaning
When Ekpe dances in Calabar
twigs of Akoko in hand
still above water

the right & left arm & leg crisscross
        alternating forward
    the shoulders inching forward
masked
    wide-eyed
        with staff sensing its way like whiskers
            hiding in deep ambush
        never divulging where her children sleep—
            while her children dress in secret cloth
            while the growl becomes visual
            while bonkó nshemiyá, the kushiyeremá
                the echo of goatskin on skin
            the growl becomes visual
Ekpe dances in Calabar
her children dressed in Ukara cloth tied secretly
    (indigo dye written with abstract paws)

They arrive in hollowed trunk
draped in palm fronds to signal sacred
The Ekóngo topped with brim hat
        pours libation of gin
        on the stone riverbank
    while the growl becomes visual
        though they say across the water
Ekpe cannot cross water

Ekpe dances in Regla también
writing the body magic
    (nsibidi they say
if you can read gesture)
like Mokóngo used to
topped with brim hat
    drinking hot drink

a blade of raffia circling his neck
      gold tooth glistening—

The story will sing forever deep
      across water
           beyond geography
      into the lushness of history—
      Ngbe!

Calabar-Miami, 2001

GLOSSARY

This is a partial glossary of some of the Spanish (specifically Cuban Spanish), Yorùbá, and other non-English words contained in this book. I chose these words because I found them important to making sense of individual poems. Words that do not appear in the glossary are either easily enough understood from the context, are used in a musical way, or are words that may remain a mystery to the reader unless they do some additional research. Readers, if you are unfamiliar with Spanish, you may find it useful to keep a Spanish/English dictionary as company.

Note on tones: Using the do, re, mi tone scale, the following symbols should be employed: ` = do   no tone= re   ´ = mi

                       o̩ = bought   e̩ = bed

Abikú: (Yor.) A child who dies in infancy or very young. It is thought that a spirit called **Emere,** who is the child's spiritual double, recalls the child back to the spirit world. Elaborate rituals and markings are performed to prevent this as well as to recognize the child when he reincarnates. Abikú are thought to be born with very distinct markings on their bodies.

Aguardiente: (Span.) Strong alcohol distilled from sugarcane.

Agwe: (Fon) Deity in the Vodún religion related to the ocean.

Akoko: A sacred herb.

Alágbede̩: (Yor.) Blacksmith.

Albahaca: (Span.) Basil.

Àràbà: Ceiba tree. Also Kapok tree.

Arará: (Fon) Descendants of Dahomeian/Fon in Cuba.

Areyto/Areito: (Taino) Ball game played by Indians. Also the field where it is played.

Asere Ekpe Muñongo Efo: (Cuban Abakua) Brother, member of the Ekpe Society lodge Muñongo Efo.

Asibong Ekondo: (Efik) Important historical figure in the Efik area of Obutong in Calabar, Nigeria.

Awó: (Yor.) Mystery. Also short for Babalawo.

Babalawo: (Yor.) Priests of Ifá/Òrúnmìlà who specialize in the knowledge of Ifá; and are thought to be the elders of Òrìshà religion.

Bacalao: (Span.) Salted codfish.

Bacalaitos: (Span.) In Puerto Rico, fritters of salted codfish.

Balafon: Wooden vibraphone from Africa.

Balsas: (Span.) Inner tubes, or dinghy crafts perilously used by Cubans to escape Cuba.

Bàtá: (Yor.)Yorùbá/Lukumí hourglass-shaped bimembranous ceremonial drums that include the okonkolú, itótele, iyá ilú.

Barbacoa: (Span./Taino) An improvised loft, second story built on an existing structure.

Bembé: (Yor.) Type of drum used in ceremonies and secular festivities. Also a party where drums are played.

Botón de oro: (Span.) Tropical herb used often in ceremonies.

Bonkó nshemiyá, the kushiyeremá: Drums in Cuban Abakua ensemble.

Cajónes: (Span.) Skinless drums made from wooden boxes. The first cajónes are thought to have been made from boxes of salted codfish.

Caribs: Tribe of Indians who were considered warriors. Descendants of these are still present in the Caribbean and South America.

Ceiba: (Span.) Silk-cotton tree. Large tropical tree thought to be the abode of many spirits. In Yorùbá called Àràbà.

Chancleta: (Span.) Slippers, flip-flops.

Clave: The basic underlying rhythm in Latin and African music. Also a pair of sticks used to play the clave beat.

Corojo: (Span.) Palm seeds from which palm oil is extracted.

Dambala: (Fon/Haitian) Deity similar to the Yorùbá Ọbatálà.

Ẹfun: (Yor.) Special white chalk for ritual use.

Èjì Ẹlẹ́mẹ̀rè: (Yor.) Two Emèrè. Also a chapter from the Ifá corpus.

Ekóngo: (Efik, Efut) Titled chief in the Ekpe society. This title in Cuba is called Mokóngo.

Ekpe: Spirit worshiped by Efik, Efat, Ejagham cultures in the Calabar area of Nigeria. It is personified by a leopard.

Epo mà l'èrò . . . : (Yor.) Palm oil will calm.

Elegba/Èshù Òdàrà: (Yor.) The messenger deity who frequently inhabits the crossroads. He is the intermediary between humans, the deities, and God.

Erzuli/Ezuli: (Haitian/Fon) Deity similar to Ọ̀shun in Vodún religion.

Èshù Òdàrà ibà re . . . : (Yor.) Incantation prior to divination greeting Elegba, and asking Ọrúnmìlà to speak the truth.

Gandó: Signatures written with chalk in Abakuá rituals.

Guanábana: (Span.) Sweet tropical fruit.

Ibo: Ethnic group in Nigeria.

Ifá: (Yor.) The Yorùbá divination oracle. There are 16 major Odù Ifá, and out of these, 240 additional Odù called ọmọlú are derived. Each Odù has countless verses, proverbs, narratives, medicines, and rituals. Much of Yorùbá culture and religion is based on Ifá.

Ifá ni Èròmásunká: (Yor.) Ifá says Èròmásunká (an odù that calls for calm and peace).

Ikin: (Yor.) Ritually prepared specialized palm nuts used during Ifá divination.

Ikírí adá Òg̣ún . . . : (Yor.) From a chant to Òg̣ún referring to his dexterity in using a sword.

Iroko: (Yor.) Deity that inhabits the giant Iroko tree.

Irosùn méjì: (Yor.) One of the 16 major Odù of Ifá.

Iyálode alade oyin: (Yor.) Iyálode (Ọ̀shun) owner of the crown of honey.

Kongo Biriyumba: An ethnic group among the Kongo.

Lengua de vaca: (Span.) Bromeliad type of plant.

Loa: (Haitian) Spirits in Vodún.

Lukumí: (Yor.) Yorùbá slaves and their descendants that populated Cuba. Also the Yorùbá dialect spoken in Cuba and the diaspora that has elements of Spanish.

Máríwò: (Yor.) Palm fronds, raffia.

Mókogún: (Yor.) An tropical herb attributed to Ògún.

Monina: (Abakna Cuba) Brother.

Nana Burukú: (Yor.) Deity related to rivers and lagoons. Close relation to Obatálà and Òshun.

Neneké: (Efik) Mythological daughter of an Efik king who founded Ekpe society.

Nganga: (Kongo) Something powerful. A receptacle where something powerful is kept.

ni jé bé: Is like this.

Nishe Òsàyìn: (Yor.) Amulet, talisman.

Nkama: (Abakuá in Cuba) Speak.

Nkaniká: (Efik) Bell, or gong.

Nsibidi: (Efik / Efut / Ejagham) Signatures, sacred writings used in Ekpe societies. In Cuba it is called Gandó.

Obatálà: (Yor.) The deity of peace, tranquility, and creation. He molds human beings while in utero. The deity that first settled the earth and prepared it for human habitation.

Odù: (Yor.) The various chapters from the Ifá oracle. Also the deity who was Òrúnmìlà's mythological wife.

Ògún: (Yor.) The deity of metals, war, hunt, and technology. In Yorùbá mythology, he opened the path so the other deities could come to earth from the spirit world.

Ògúndá kara wá . . . : (Yor.) From a chant to Ògún referring to his omnipresence.

Ògúndá: (Yor.) One of the 16 major Odù Ifá containing many verses regarding Ògún.

Ọ̀kànràn: (Yor.) A configuration in the coconut, kola nuts, cowry divination, and one of the 16 major Odù Ifá.

Olókun: (Yor.) The deity that reigns over the oceans and all bodies of water thought to live in the depths of the ocean.

Olórun: Owner of the sun, sky. God.

Ọmọlú: One of 240 Odù Ifá. Literally "child of king." Offspring of 16 major Odù Ifá.

Oríkí: (Yor.) Praise poem, reserved for praising deities, important people, families.

Òrìshà: (Yor.) Deity, gods, goddesses.

Ọrúnmìlà: (Yor.) The deity of wisdom, knowledge, oratory, and divination. Master of the Ifá oracle.

Ọ̀shun: (Yor.) The female deity of fertility, fresh water, arts, and patron of women. Also a river in Nigeria.

Oyibo: (Yor.) White man.

Palo Moruro: (Span.) Tree whose very red trunk is thought to have medicinal and spiritual properties.

Pèrègún: (Yor.) Very important ceremonial herb.

Piropos: (Span.) Witty compliments men say to women in Caribbean environs.

Quiebra Hacha: (Span.) "Breaks an axe." A hardwood tree.

Quimbombo: (Span.) Okra.

Repique: (Span.) Drum solo, drum roll usually on a conga drum.

San Lao . . . : Pidgin Spanish song dedicated to San Lazaro (Saint Lazarus).

Sarabanda Kimbansa: Deity in the Kongo religion, similar to Ògún.

Shangó: (Yor.) Deity of thunder, lightning, and bàtá drums. Also the historical 4th Alafin (King) of Oyó, Nigeria.

Siguaraya: The national tree of Cuba. A hardwood.

Spiritize: The jazzy spiritualization of matter.

Sunkún: (Yor.) Crying.

Taino: Tribe of Indians from precolonial Cuba and Puerto Rico. They were very peaceful and welcoming. They were decimated by violence and disease soon after colonialism began.

Timbal: (Span.) Timpani-type drums used in Latin music.

Ukara: (Efik) Type of indigo dyed cloth used by Ekpe society members.

Uságare: Region in western Nigeria near the Cameroon border. Also the name of an Ekpe society in Cuba.

Vacuna: The act of when a man imitates a rooster courting a hen while dancing rumba, but *not* Yambú, another dance.

Vodún: (Haitian/Fon) Deity, gods, goddesses.

Yambú: (Span.) One of three genres of rumba in Cuban music. Yambú is played with cajónes and its pace is much slower than the other genres of guaguancó and columbia.

Yemojá: (Yor.) The female deity of oceans and motherhood.

Yorùbá: Ethnic group in West Africa (now southwestern Nigeria) from which many slaves were captured and brought to the Caribbean. A major influence in Cuban culture. Their descendants continued their traditions and manifested it into "Regla de Ocha," the most predominant of Afro-Cuban religions. Today the Yorùbá number in the millions and are spread around the globe. Although greatly influenced by colonialism, Christianity, and Islam, many continue to practice their traditional religion and culture.

COLOPHON

Wise Fish was designed at Coffee House Press
in the Warehouse District of downtown Minneapolis.
Poems are set in Spectrum; titles in Blakely Light.

FUNDER ACKNOWLEDGMENTS

Coffee House Press is an independent nonprofit literary publisher. Our books are made possible through the generous support of grants and gifts from many foundations, corporate giving programs, individuals, and through state and federal support. Coffee House Press receives general operating support from the Minnesota State Arts Board, through an appropriation by the Minnesota State Legislature and from the National Endowment for the Arts, a federal agency. Coffee House receives major funding from the McKnight Foundation, and from Target. Coffee House also receives significant support from: an anonymous donor; the Buuck Family Foundation; the Bush Foundation; the Patrick and Aimee Butler Family Foundation; Consortium Book Sales and Distribution; the Foundation for Contemporary Performance Arts; Stephen and Isabel Keating; the Lerner Family Foundation; the Outagamie Foundation; the Pacific Foundation; the law firm of Schwegman, Lundberg, Woessner & Kluth, P.A.; the James R. Thorpe Foundation; West Group; the Woessner Freeman Family Foundation; and many other generous individual donors.

This activity is made possible in part by a grant from the Minnesota State Arts Board, through an appropriation by the Minnesota State Legislature and a grant from the National Endowment for the Arts.

MINNESOTA
STATE ARTS BOARD

NATIONAL
ENDOWMENT
FOR THE ARTS

To you and our many readers across the country,
we send our thanks for your continuing support.

Good books are brewing at coffeehousepress.org